THE WINTER WIZARD

Sam Retallick was born in Cornwall, and has never left. He graduated from Falmouth University with a BA(hons) in Creative Writing. His in progress novel, *Octobaby*, was one of two entrants recognised as 'highly commended' in the Writers and Artists Working-Class-Writers' Prize 2022. *The Winter Wizard* is his first book.

© 2025, Sam Retallick. All rights reserved; no part of this book may be reproduced by any means without the publisher's permission.

ISBN: 978-1-917617-26-0

The author has asserted their right to be identified as the author of this Work in accordance with the Copyright, Designs and Patents Act 1988

Cover designed by Aaron Kent

Edited and Typeset by Aaron Kent

Broken Sleep Books Ltd
PO BOX 102
Llandysul
SA44 9BG

CONTENTS

I	9
A SUMMONING SPELL	11
III	12
BOBBIN FOUND	13
V	15
VI	16
BOBBIN LOST	17
VIII	18
IX	19
X	20
EQUINOXE	21
ACKNOWLEDGEMENTS	25

The Winter Wizard

Sam Retallick

Broken Sleep Books

I see a friend,
Coming down the gutter,
'Hawthorne! Hayseed! Mildew!'
Under his breath, he mutters

He twists and contorts,
Past spider and lichen,
His bones become wicker,
And softer than elder

Then he shoots from the spout,
All purple and muddled,
Beard in a tangle,
And all of a hurry

'St Nicholas has gone,'
he says, brushing brambles from whiskers
'And Spring Lamb, still she slumbers.'
As he balances hat,
Upon noble features

'Fine lad, you're now in the care
of The Winter Wizard.'

And winking one purple eye,
Scampers into the bushes,
Lithe as a lizard.

I

He is spoken of in pubs
And taverns,
With dark wood floors and bowed ceilings
In closed conversation
And Sanskrit whispers

They know his name on the moorland,
Amongst granite and scrub,
Say he was born on the gasps of a scirocco

They know him in the docks,
Amongst dead fish and rusted iron,
Rough men and rougher weather,
In underground dive bars
Damp cellars
Say he was born inside a mk2 Volkswagen Scirocco

I've known him in the woods,
Under each fragrant needle or decomposing cone,
Taste his breath on my skin,
His broth on my lips

Some know him in tiled bathrooms
Stained with grime and stank of piss

Have knelt at his altar
Found warmth from his gifts

When Michaelmas has faded,
And St Nicholas fled,
He comes

He nurtures snowdrops at the tips of his fingers,
Blesses discarded pines and unloved kin alike,
He walks amongst the dark, the cold, the broken and bracken

And until spring arrives
We are all in the care of the Winter Wizard.

A SUMMONING SPELL

Cloak of purple on crescent moon,
Sleeping child,
Broken spoon,

Beard of white and eyes of aster,
Bring forth dildos, rocks and plaster

Scream into your pillow,
Or bite on your thumb
Bless the broken-down buses
With discount-price rum

Wizard!
Hear me, and open thy arms
Block out the chill,
Bestill what's not calm
Come dark clouds and rainbow
And conical hat
Bring thy bobbin and fairies
Trample codfish and cat

III

In France they call you Pavlug,
A mischievous goblin
Who treads long unkempt hair
By means of a warning

And you keep by your side
An enchanted old bobbin
With Bavarian flair
And the cry of a Robin

BOBBIN FOUND

Bristol born on the Tamar,

Watching the jetsam

Flow from

    Devon

  to

Cornwall

I saw you

Your chipped varnish

Lightwood curves

Painted beak and red breast,

Knew you were worth saving

Discarded coat,

Warmth,

And leapt

into waters brown,

Swam to salvage

Your bent pins

Floating body

Kissed your sewage-tasting shape

Brought you back

With lips that tickled the fae

And bound us

My soul to yours

A boy and his bobbin

V

I danced amongst the willows again last night

Saw the moon through tired eyes

Felt fingerprints burn into my

Back

Thighs

Wrists

Skin

I danced amongst the toadstools and the valerian

Ate moss and aniseed

And no one but the toads heard my tears

I walked with the badger, the fox and oxen made of stars

They showed me hidden graves,

Dormice and roadkill

I danced under the willow

But it was dying

I kissed its bark

Smoothed its leaves

Whispered a salve

Then hopped the barbed wire

Back to my nest.

VI

I can fold a piece of paper

I can fold a whole and make two halves

I can fold fish,

Turn scale to scale

Gill to tail

And gaze into black empty eyes

I can fold metal into points

Cragged and hard

Can drive needles into meat

Death throes into ecstasy

But I cannot fold a person

Nor a partridge

Nor a book

And so I fold and deliver

Fold and deliver

BOBBIN LOST

When the Wizard was young,
And full of ideas,
He built a small village
Based on Bognor Regis.

He built a viaduct for ants
A carousel for lice
He captured the rodents,
Made horses of mice.

His Knitting Doll was king, up high in the priory
He oversaw rain, sleet and snow
Without comment or irony.

When the Knitting Doll was lost,
The Wizard grew mad,
Burst the banks of the viaduct,
Squashed lice beneath hand.

The knitting Doll knew
The knitting Doll fled
Threw himself to the river,
Left love for dead.

VIII

Spring sunshine

And the watery heat

warms bones,

Thaws frost from deep joints

Promises greenery and birdsong

IX

Amongst the pampas grass and dunes

I first saw an adder

Marvelled at red eyes

Diamond danger

The promise of venom

I crept away

Let you rest

Until spring you must slumber

I walked back up the path,

Gathered pebbles,

And watched where I tread.

X

Wet leaves stick to my feet
I am awoken, alone, once more under pine tree
Nightmusic fills me, Cry of Bat, Yelp of Fox, Hoot of
Tawny owl
Elegiac and solitary

Rabbits scamper around my bare legs, fur slick with morning dew,
White with shock

Ivy on the breeze,
A change is coming

A rustle, a whistle, a bang
And we are galloping,
Over stile,
Through mud,
Beasts of the night.

EQUINOXE

March arrives

The snowdrops have company in the verges

And lone pheasants' fields are overrun with songbirds,

Spindle-boned and sinewy boys

Brush off leaf litter

Lichen

Root and sycamore seed

The mole burrows shallow

The footsteps form on hardened mud

And the Winter Wizard must leave

He comes for his doll,

His boy,

His bobbin,

And I kiss you once more

Return my soul to this realm

And the magic leaves me.

His hands are gnarled and ashen,

His snowdrops have wilted

His beard is full of bones,

Tiny,

delicate,

Sharp

He will return,

Beard, Bobbin and conical hat

But for now,

It is spring,

And the willow calls me,

Not dying,

But radiant.

ACKNOWLEDGEMENTS

Thank-you to my parents, Aunty, Selina & Zoe for your unwavering support, and to the great teachers of my life, Chris, Meredith & Frea for your encouragement and enthusiasm.

LAY OUT YOUR UNREST

www.ingramcontent.com/pod-product-compliance
Lightning Source LLC
LaVergne TN
LVHW041313080426
835510LV00009B/971